LEARN TO DRAW... PRINCESS KINGDOM!

By Mara Conlon

Illustrated by Kerren Barbas Steckler

Designed by Heather Zschock

PETER PAUPER PRESS, INC.

White Plains, New York

For Emily and Audrey

PETER PAUPER PRESS

In 1928, at the age of twenty-two, Peter Beilenson began printing books on a small press in the basement of his parents' home in Larchmont, New York. Peter—and later, his wife, Edna—sought to create fine books that sold at "prices even a pauper could afford."

Today, still family owned and operated, Peter Pauper Press continues to honor our founders' legacy of quality, value, and fun for big kids and small kids alike.

Illustrations copyright © 2015 Kerren Barbas Steckler

Designed by Heather Zschock

Copyright © 2015
Peter Pauper Press, Inc.
Manufactured for Peter Pauper Press, Inc.
202 Mamaroneck Avenue
White Plains, NY 10601
ISBN 978-1-4413-0558-9
Printed in China

Published in the United Kingdom and Europe by
Peter Pauper Press Inc. c/o White Pebble International
Unit 2, Plot 11 Terminus Road
Chichester, West Sussex PO19 8TX, UK
7 6 5 4 3 2 1

Visit us at www.peterpauper.com

Hey, young artists!

Are you ready to learn how to draw 47 different magical princess pictures? It's easy and fun! Just follow these steps:

· ·

First, pick a royal picture you want to draw. (You might want to start with the tiara . . . it's pretty simple, and regal!)

Next, trace over the picture with a pencil. This will give you a feel for how to draw the lines.

Then, following the numbered boxes, start drawing each new step (shown in red) of the picture in the empty space in each scene, or on a piece of paper.

Lastly, if you're an awesome artist (and of course, you are!), try drawing a whole fairy tale scene with one or more of these majestic things. And remember, don't worry if your drawings look different from the ones in this book—no two princesses, bouquets, or magic mirrors are exactly alike!

You are well on your way to creating enchanting masterpieces!

GET READY! GET SET! DRAW!

Hat

1.

2.

3.

Tiara

1.

2.

3.

4.

Dress

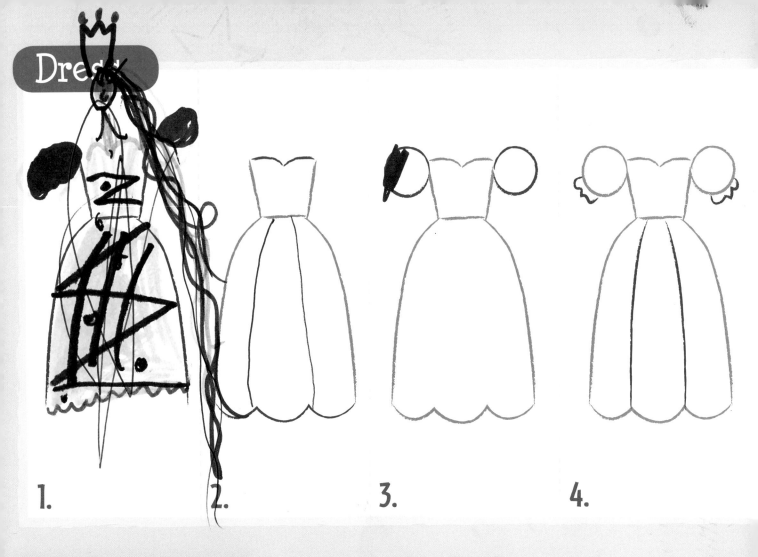

1.   2.   3.   4.

Prince outfit

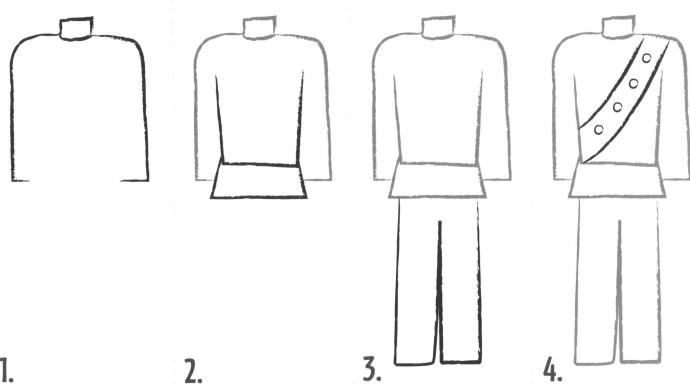

1.   2.   3.   4.

Trace over me for practice!

Princess

1.

2.

3.

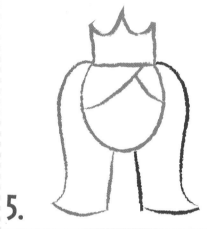

4.

5.

6.

Prince

1.

2.

3.

4.

5.

6.

Frog

1.

2.

3.

4.

5.

6.

Dragonfly

1.

2.

3.

4.

5.

Draw more like me below!

Castle

1.

2.

3.

4.

5.

6.

Rosebush

1.

2.

3.

4.

5.

6.

Ring and bracelet

 1.

 2.

 3.

 1.

2.

 3.

Jewelry box

 1.

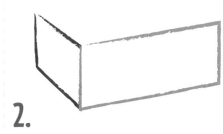 2.

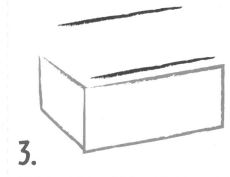 3.

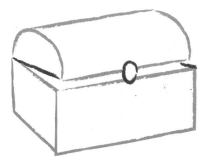 4.

5.

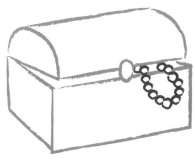 6.

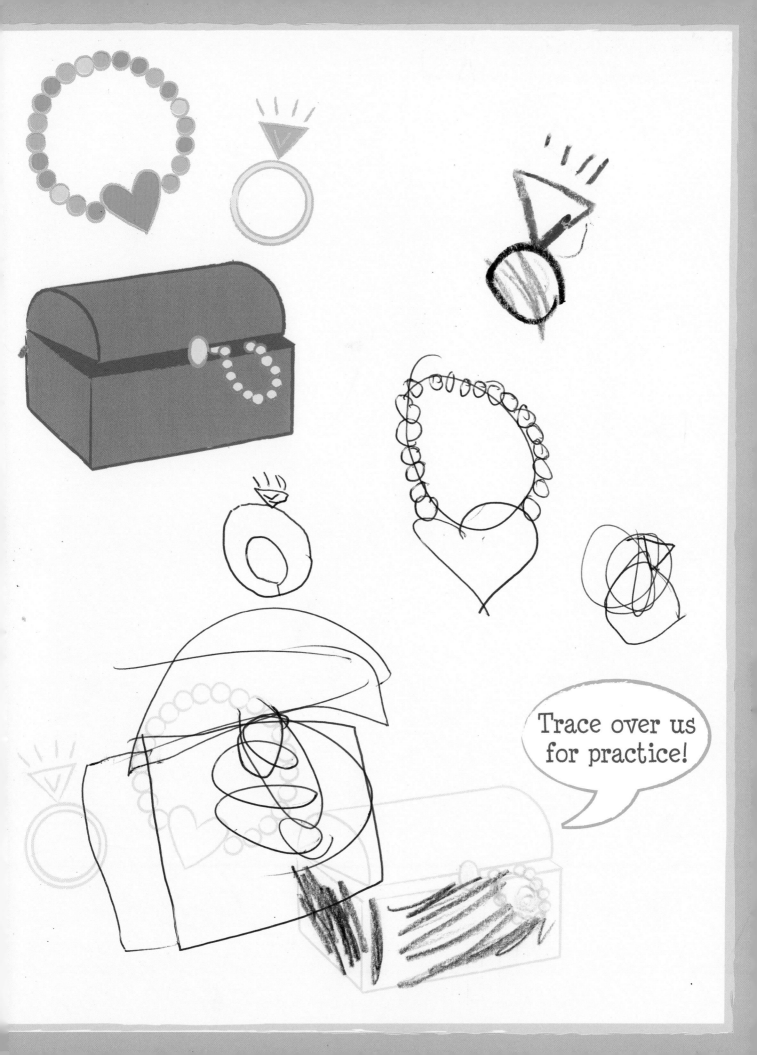

Trace over us
for practice!

Rose

1. 2. 3. 4. 5. 6.

Bouquet

1. 2. 3.

4. 5. 6.

Butterfly

1.

2.

3.

4.

5.

6.

Bird

1.

2.

3.

4.

5.

6.

Crown

1.

2.

3.

4.

5.

6.

Royal crown

1.

2.

3.

4.

5.

6.

Carriage

1.

2.

3.

4.

5.

6.

Horse

1.

2.

3.

4.

5.

6.

King

1.

2.

3.

4.

5.

6.

Scepter

1.

2.

3.

4.

Queen's dress

1.

2.

3.

4.

Queen's robe

1.

2.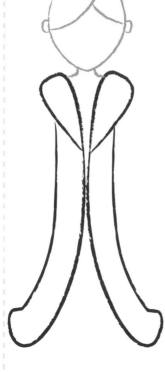

3.

4.

Unicorn

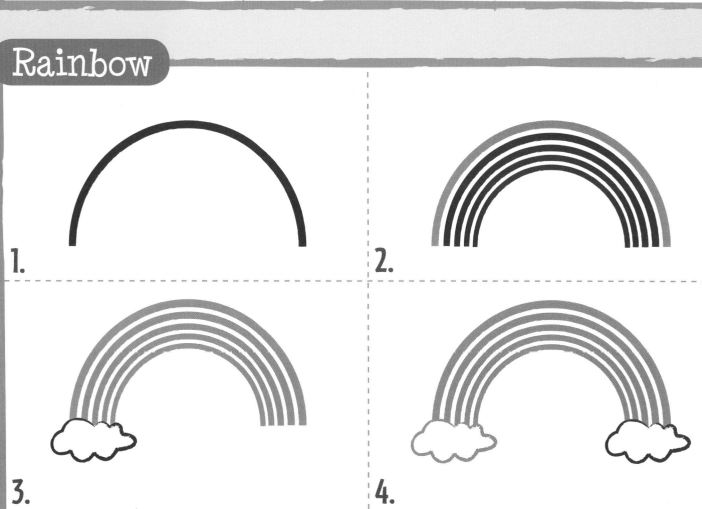

1.

2.

3.

4.

5.

6.

Rainbow

1.

2.

3.

4.

Trace over me
for practice!

Wand

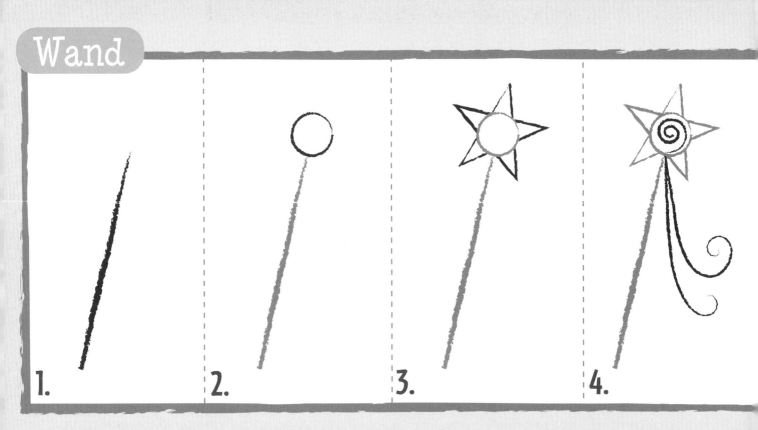

1.

2.

3.

4.

Fairy Godmother

1.

2.

3.

4.

5.

6.

Draw more like
me above!

Sword & shield

1.

2.

3.

1.

2.

3.

Knight

1.

2.

3.

4.

Throne

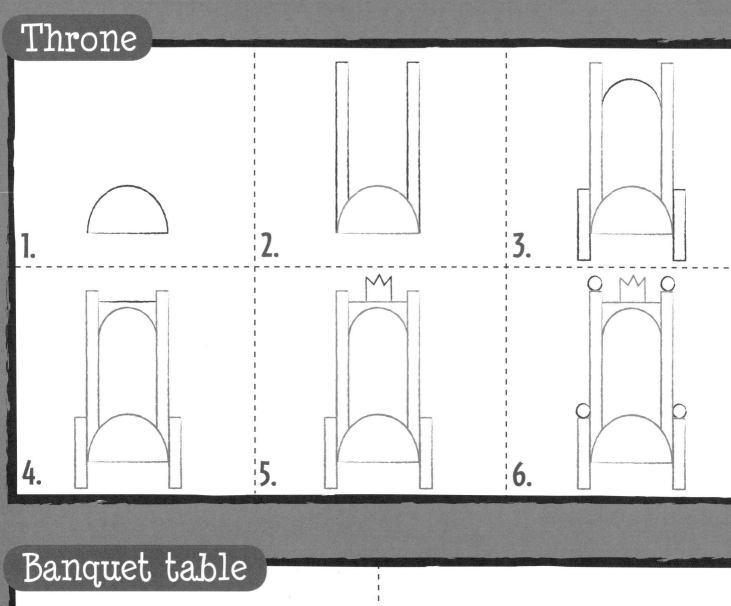

1.

2.

3.

4.

5.

6.

Banquet table

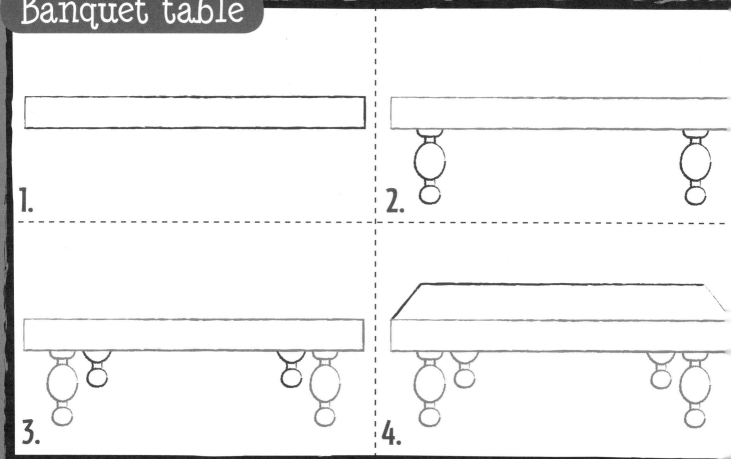

1.

2.

3.

4.

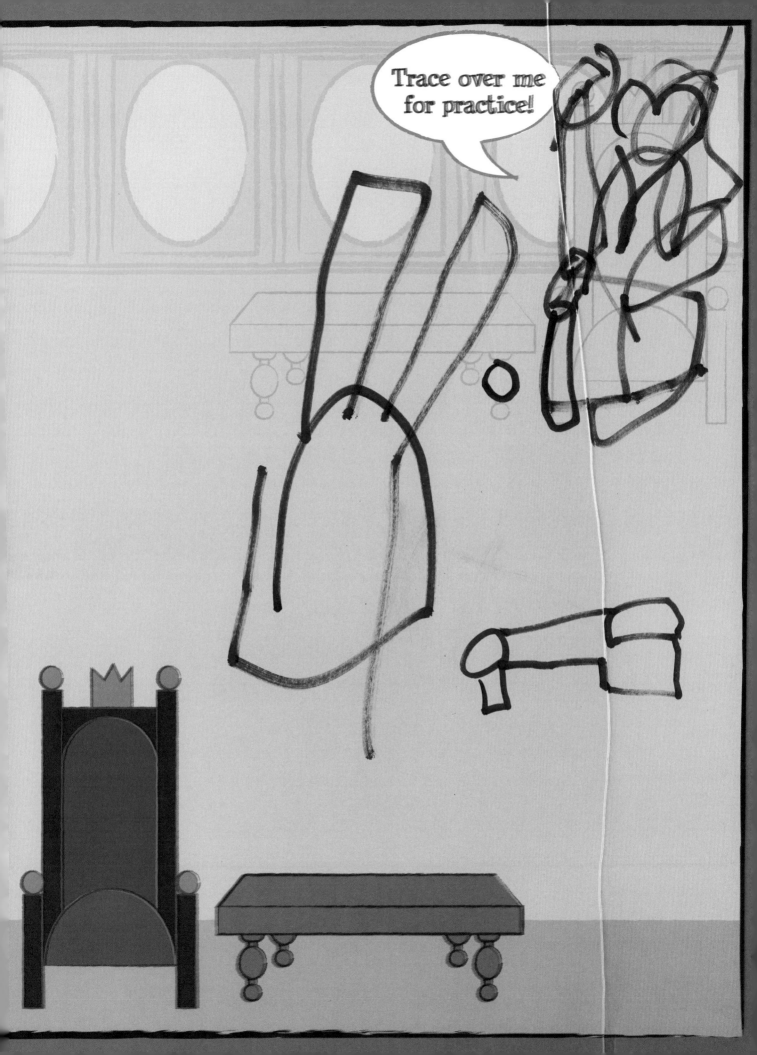

Mirror

1.

2.

3.

4.

Perfume

1.

2.

3.

4.

Makeup

1.

2.

3.

4.

Swan

1.

2.

3.

4.

5.

6.

Bridge

1.

2.

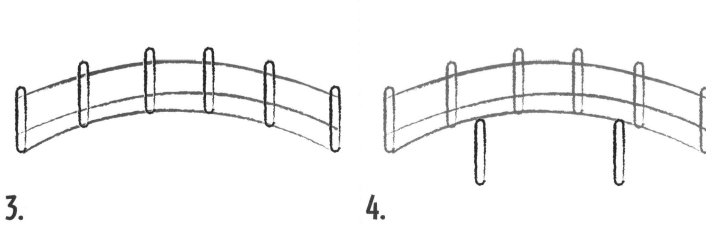

3.

4.

Dragon

1.

2.

3.

4.

5.

6.

Wizard

1.

2.

3.

4.

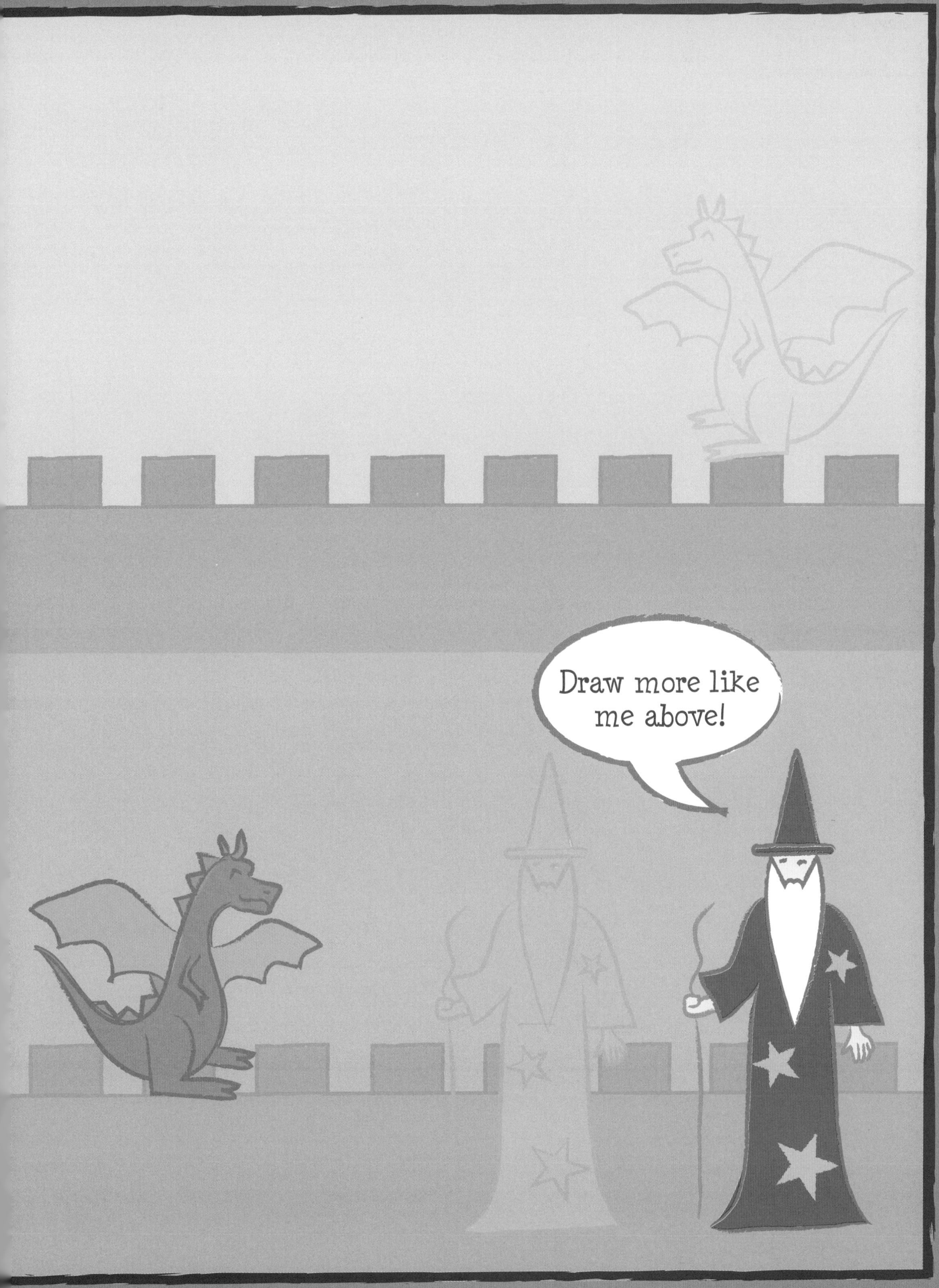
Draw more like me above!

Cauldron

1.

2.

3.

4.

5.

6.

Witch

1.

2.

3.

4.

Trace over me for practice!

Rabbit

1.

2.

3.

4.

5.

6.

Squirrel

1.

2.

3.

4.

5.

6.

Glass slipper

1.

2.

3.

4.

5.

6.

Gloves

1.

2.

3.

Trace over me for practice!

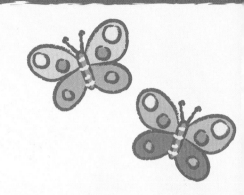

Rolling hills and castles,
kings and queens,
butterflies and royal frogs...

How will YOU draw your
princess scene?